The Core Value
Proposition

Capture the power of your business building ideas!

A powerful anchor and new starting point for innovative business development

Jack G. Hardy

v.1.0

Note for Librarians: a cataloguing record for this book that includes Dewey Decimal Classification and US Library of Congress numbers is available from the Library and Archives of Canada. The complete cataloguing record can be obtained from their online database at:
www.collectionscanada.ca/amicus/index-e.html
ISBN 1-4120-4937-7
Printed in Victoria, BC, Canada

TRAFFORD

Offices in Canada, USA, Ireland, UK and Spain
This book was published *on-demand* in cooperation with Trafford Publishing. On-demand publishing is a unique process and service of making a book available for retail sale to the public taking advantage of on-demand manufacturing and Internet marketing. On-demand publishing includes promotions, retail sales, manufacturing, order fulfilment, accounting and collecting royalties on behalf of the author.
Book sales for North America and international:
Trafford Publishing, 6E–2333 Government St.,
Victoria, BC V8T 4P4 CANADA
phone 250 383 6864 (toll-free 1 888 232 4444)
fax 250 383 6804; email to orders@trafford.com
Book sales in Europe:
Trafford Publishing (UK) Ltd., Enterprise House, Wistaston Road Business Centre,
Wistaston Road, Crewe, Cheshire CW2 7RP UNITED KINGDOM
phone 01270 251 396 (local rate 0845 230 9601)
facsimile 01270 254 983; orders.uk@trafford.com
Order online at:
www.trafford.com/robots/04-2745.html

10 9 8 7 6 5 4 3 2

Contents

My name is Jack Hardy: I'm a marketing guy, a seminar leader, a business consultant and an ex-CEO. Recently I took on the task of reexamining business-building innovation.

Experience told me..."People succeed at creating a prosperous and profitable business because — *either knowingly or intuitively* — they define their business development activities in terms of *fundamental core values*."

Could I prove this theory in practice?

Could I define these fundamental core values?

The *traditional* business plan

In a recent survey of *Inc.* magazine's 500 founders, one question asked whether they had written formal business plans *before* they launched their companies. Only 40% said yes. Of those, 65% said they had strayed significantly from their original idea, adapting their plans as they went along. And only 12% said they'd done formal market research.

Only 2 out of 10 wrote a formal business plan before they launched their companies. Their business plan was well researched and tailored to sell their idea to investors. They were raising money to invest in assets. Be sure, this business plan was all-inclusive and required a major investment of time and money.

All others – 8 out of 10 – strayed significantly from their original conception, *adapting* their plans as they went along. They built their business within a *more fluid, less structured* form of planning. There was no evidence of a common use of *core values*.

There's more: The Global Entrepreneurship Monitor reports that in the United States some 11% of the working population are either running a young business – less than 3 years old – or are actively trying to start one.

That means as many as 20 million prospective entrepreneurs are at work. Subtract "wishful thinkers," and that's still a gigantic group. And, it doesn't include all those working on new products with an established company.

As a result, seminars and workshops on how to write a business plan have become something of a crutch. The Internet is flooded with "quick fix" easy-to-do *traditional* business plan solutions: from software packages, checklists and outlines, to just what the doctor ordered "cookie cutter" plans, some even customized by industry category.

In fact, there hasn't been much guidance or reflection given to business building other than the *traditional* business plan format.

CATCH-22: The dilemma...

The experts – academics, bankers and consultants – *recommend* the traditional business plan as the best starting point for business development.

But those who succeed in starting or building a business find the traditional business plan's myriad details overwhelming, much too time consuming. They find their way through a *more fluid, less structured* format.

The Core Value Proposition started with 7 facts...

1. **Innovation feeds upon Ideas.** Starting or growing an existing business *begins* with the talent to detect, create, select and define viable new business ideas. Search the marketplace for opportunities, perhaps inconsistent customer behavior.

Innovation is powered by convictions born from an idea's core values.

2. **Everything in business starts (or stops) with the customer.** The more you know about the customer, the more likely it is you can offer the right product, at the right time, at the right place with the right price.

Innovative thinking builds an organization's "new idea" inventory.

3. **Business growth depends upon innovative thinking:** New ideas frequently confront an established and sometimes daunting development process. A comfortable, stress-free ongoing innovative process helps motivate people.

Powerful ideas attract outstanding people create loyalty and dedication.

4. **Focus is critical to business development:** The most effective route is to select and focus upon that one idea that can be projected to grow your core business.

Develop one idea at a time; beware of the unfamiliar.

5. **Resources are always limited:** Big company or small, day-to-day pressures limit the amount of time and money dedicated to new idea development. Small business folks have a built-in advantage over a larger business. It's easier for them to experiment and explore, detect and create new ideas. Big

business emphasis is on market detection and segment selection rather than new segment creation.

A concise well-defined innovative process maximizes resources.

6. **Beware the Flash of Genius!** "Hey, I've got a great idea!" All too frequently this is the starting point for business innovation. No time for planning. But, without the foundation of a solid, compelling customer oriented strategy...98% fail!

Innovation is built upon what customers need, not "gut feeling."

7. **Innovation is always a possibility!** Some organizations reach a stage of development where margins are relentlessly squeezed. Products or services are considered simply as commodities, sensitive *only* to price. The ability to create change is overpowered by management's "iron clad" attitude: innovation is impossible! But the truth is...

Without innovative thinking organizations eventually wither and die. The only institution that successfully rejects change is the cemetery!

Catch-22: The dilemma is solved!

A recent study of effective management practices[*] concluded that innovation works effectively if its strategy is built[*] around a clear *value proposition for the customer.* It must be sharply defined, clearly communicated, and well understood by employees, customers, owners and investors.

---

[*] What Really Works, Harvard Business Review, Reprint R0307C

This was the last clue needed to identify the Core Value Proposition; connect it to 5 Value Drivers and setup a simple, easy to use 4-step planning process. Together this process provides a customer oriented solution to innovative thinking, business planning and development.

+--------------------------------------+---------------------------+
The Core Value	A powerful anchor and
Proposition	new starting point for
	innovative business
	development
+--------------------------------------+---------------------------+

"You cannot discover new oceans unless you have the courage to lose sight of the shore." – Unknown

What is your business-building objective?

Refocus your business to restore growth? Create a new product or service? Start a new company? Increase sales and profits? Or is it personal? Illuminate your personal career path? Grow into a better job? The Core Value Proposition will work for you with each one of these tasks...*and many more!*

The Core Value Proposition introduces a more powerful anchor, a new starting point within an easy to understand 4-step business-building process:

- **Detect, create and select** new and viable innovative business building ideas.

- **Create a Core Value Proposition** – Use 5 Value Drivers to define the Idea's core values.

- **Prove the Core Value Proposition** is viable – Give life to the idea! Is it *financially workable?*

- **Create a compelling business plan.** Use the Core Value Proposition as its nexus – tailor its content to a specific communications purpose.

The process begins with an Idea. Your ability to detect, create, select and define viable new business ideas. Then, each **Value Driver** gives body to the Idea by clearly revealing specific *core values.*

These 5 questions define each Value Driver...

- **IDEA:** What does your product or service idea **DO** for your Customers?
    Put yourself in the Customer's place.

- **BENEFIT:** How do your Customers **benefit** from your IDEA**?**
    Think like a Customer Is there something unique? Better than the competition?

- **TARGET:** How can Customers be **identified** separately from others? How can they be reached?

- **PERCEPTION:** How do YOU want to be **perceived**? By your customers? By the public? By your employees?

- **REWARD:** What's in it for you? Your partners? Stockholders? Employees?

Developing the **5 Value Drivers** forms a systematic process for gathering information and experience. Long term, each is a continuing source of strength, growth and renewal for your company's products and services.

When the **5 Value Drivers** are woven together, they create the **Core Value Proposition**.

The **Core Value Proposition** and its **5 Value Drivers** provide a simplified, more fluid form of planning. Its techniques provide synergy to the dynamics of developing a successful business. The process generates power to grow a business with products and services that are *competitively unique*.

The **Core Value Proposition** fine-tunes a business-building strategy and becomes the nexus or center of a compelling business plan. In practice the **Core Value**

Proposition becomes a *living force* that casts it influence upon all phases of the organization's activity.

The **Core Value Proposition** provides a tight focus to the evaluation process that proves its viability. Proof is doable rapidly, reducing the risk of lost opportunities. This real life substantiation provides the experience upon which a compelling business plan is built.

Over the course of this past year, I've tested and proven Value Drivers in numerous business-building seminars. I confirmed how easily most participants understand the context of each Value Driver.

Some, however, treat the 5 Drivers casually, as superficial statements. Others grasp the profound significance of each Value Driver. They relentlessly pursue its all-embracing borders to gain both information and experience.

CAUTION! **Learn to think like a Customer!** Everything starts *(or stops)* with the Customer.

Defining a Value Driver means you *must* learn to think like a Customer. This cuts out theory and captures reality.

Peter Drucker, in his book *Management Challenges for the 21st Century*, established this point-of-view... "The foundations of management have to be customer values and customer decisions on the distribution of their disposable income."

Business Week magazine recently noted, "Behind every BW50 success story there's usually a company culture that encourages more one-of-a-kind products or proves more adaptable than rivals, *often by learning to think like their customers.*"

Can I prove the merits of the Core Value Proposition?

I'll show you evidence, actual case stories, companies whose success is sourced from a clear Core Value Proposition...*despite their industry's circumstances.* In one case, competitors are hanging just a razor's edge away from bankruptcy.

Perhaps you're thinking, "Will I be able to relate these case stories to my own business problems?" Each story was selected to illustrate the relevance of core values to small business birth and ongoing development.

I've included two stories from the FORTUNE 500: P&G and Southwest Airlines. But both stories go back to their earliest stages, *their roots!*

In both cases, you'll find the story of how people working together with limited resources – *focused by core values* – built the foundations of a large, dynamic and innovative business.

And it's most likely you've never heard of either King Arthur Flour or Cobalt Boats — both fast growing small companies.

Both illustrate how a vibrant business is built reaching out with genuine core values to a specific and well-identified target market.

And you'll find mention of Frederick W. Smith the guy who identified and developed the opportunity to revolutionize the package delivery industry.

You'll also meet Stephen Fossler, a brilliant direct marketer who turned the idea of embossed anniversary labels into $27 million cash.

Last but not least, the owner of a six-chair barbershop – in trouble, on the verge of closing its doors – making a 12-month comeback. He focused upon customers with a simple, easy to manage database marketing technique. And he did it without a computer: just an agenda, an address book and a telephone.

Here's my promise to you:

Use the Core Value Proposition to capture the full power of your business building ideas. Work with its 5 Value Drivers to develop your business-building objectives and strategy. Your business building achievements will be more effective and enduring. You will save time and money and find greater rewards.

This Guide will help you understand how to define, state and use each Value Driver. It will show you how to weave the 5 Value Drivers into a Core Value Proposition. Then, test your idea giving proof to its viability. And, lastly, use the Core Value Proposition to create a compelling business plan.

Don't get me wrong! Certainly, you can build a workable business *without* a Core Value Proposition. *It's done every day.*

But know this: Without a Core Value Proposition, a clear distinction from your competition, most probably you'll soon be a price sensitive commodity. It's *your* choice.

• • •

Please copy and use this next page as your **Core Value Proposition Worksheet**. Prepare a new page in your computer or use a pad of paper.

TIP: A 3-ring notebook with 5 or more dividers helps keep your Value Driver development information organized.

Worksheet - Core Value Proposition

Value Drivers	☐ Company ☐ Product or Service
Idea What do we DO for the customer?	
Benefits What's in it for the customer? Compared to competition?	
Target **Who** is in the Target Market? **How** do we reach them?	
Perception How do WE want to be perceived? Customers? Employees? Suppliers?	
Reward – What's in it for us? Owner? Employees? Partners? Shareholders?	
Core Value Proposition	

```
┌─────────────────────────────┬─────────────────────────┐
│   Value Driver              │  What do you DO         │
│   The Idea                  │  for your Customers?    │
└─────────────────────────────┴─────────────────────────┘
```

A mind stretched by new ideas
never regains its original dimensions.

How to detect, create and select new business ideas?

Ideas are a possible way of doing something.

The **Idea Value Driver** asks, "What is it you DO for your Customers?" The challenge is *defining* a business building idea, an idea that has *value* for the Customer.

Building a business or a new product starts with a dream, your dream, your vision of the business or the product or service you want to create. You say, "Yes, I can *see* it! — Yes, I can *do* it!"

Simple logic declares that if you do what everyone else does, you'll get pretty much the same results. Being different often means coming up with obvious insights. Sometimes these insights foster ideas capable of turning industries upside down. They create a competitive edge. They create ideas that others will work for decades trying to copy.

As you read on, you'll come across what I call an "idea selector." It's an effective way to collect ideas. Idea selectors use a mathematical logic format, a "conditional" sentence formed by combining two thoughts (or facts) into a premise by using the words: IF and THEN.

"IF I do this THEN that will happen."

This idea selector format stimulates clear thinking when developing new business ideas. It allows you to create a network of ideas. Evaluate each set with logic, either "true" or "false."

As you develop your Value Drivers, IF the reasoning that follows supports the logic as "true," THEN your Value Drivers will connect to the Core Value Proposition.

However, IF the reasoning of your Value Driver development proves to be illogical or poorly founded, THEN your idea proves "false." That signals you to go back to the drawing board and start over.

Daring to be different: The FedEx story!

In 1965, Yale University undergraduate Frederick W. Smith wrote a term paper about the passenger route systems used by most airfreight shippers. He viewed the system as economically inadequate. Smith recognized the need for shippers to have a system that could accommodate time-sensitive shipments such as medicines, computer parts and electronics. It's said that Smith's professor didn't think much of the idea. *"Who could replace the US Postal Service?"*

In August of 1971, following a stint in the military, Smith bought controlling interest in Arkansas Aviation Sales, located in Little Rock, Arkansas. While operating his new firm, Smith identified the tremendous difficulty in getting time sensitive packages and other airfreight delivered within one to two days. This problem motivated him to do the basic research needed to define the idea, an idea that could resolve an inefficient distribution system.

His idea revolutionized global business practices and redefined delivery speed and reliability. He called it Federal Express!

Using our idea selector, a "conditional" sentence, Smith's idea could be stated:

> **IF** we create an airborne service that guarantees overnight package delivery, delivers the package on time and in good condition at a reasonable price, **THEN** people will use our service.

In 1994, taking directions from its customers, Federal Express officially adopted "FedEx" as its brand identity. Customers used the term as a verb, meaning, "to send an overnight shipment." Today it's common terminology to "FedEx" a package.

The second change came in 2000 when the company was renamed FedEx Express to reflect its position within the total FedEx Corporation portfolio of services. FedEx was no longer just an overnight delivery service.

Today, FedEx Express, the largest operating company in the FedEx family, delivers about 3.3 million packages and documents each and every business day.

FedEx is now a family of companies that offer a global network of specialized services — transportation, information, international trade support and supply chain services. More than 210,000 people put it all together every day.

Listen to your customers!

Take time to listen to your customers. Listen carefully... How does your product or service fit into their life? Have you seen this fit first-hand? What can you learn from your competitors? What are *they* doing for their customers? Can *their* ideas be a resource? Can they be *upgraded* quickly, easily and effectively? Or, can you hook your idea to a successful new product?

Learn to think like a customer!

It's not easy. Thinking like a customer takes practice. Think about your customers *and* the competition. Some call it learning to think "from outside-in." Talk with customers. Listen carefully to what they say...

A value driven idea is not necessarily what you now make or produce. When you think like a customer, you avoid being focused internally. Fred Smith was focused by his customers needs. As you examine your market from a customer's point-of-view, perhaps an entirely new process will become your dream. It's possible your value driven idea will *empower* your company with a new, long-term meaning and direction.

Hooking on to Apple Computer's iPod

Apple computer's iPod has proven a colossal hit on the electronics and entertainment market. The tiny white Apple music machine has won a fanatical following in the United States, Europe and Japan. And the iPod has opened a secondary market for an enormous quantity of accessories whose market is valued at over $50 million: carrying cases, hi-fi speakers, arm band carriers, stereo connectors...a long and fast growing list of opportunities.

"We load your iPod!" – this iPod service transfers your complete music collection to your iPod at a reasonable cost and significant time saving. Just take them your iPod and a stack of CD's. Done in a day or two. *It's now a national franchise.*

Hewlett Packard reached an agreement with Apple to sell its own version of the iPod in a wide range of retail outlets such as Costco and Office Depot. HP expanded the iPod's distribution well beyond the places where Apple currently sells the players. Good business for both.

In a new twist, HP will offer customizable "tattoos" for the iPod. Tattoos are customizable labels that it calls "HP Printable Tattoos" which allow iPod owners to put their own art, or art from musicians such as album covers, on their iPods. Users download the artwork from the www.HPshopping.com music website and print it on the tattoos. Then simply wrap the tattoo around the body of the iPod. *Cool!*

And, Apple's iPod is leading a major change in the personal computer market – opening up even more opportunities for a "hook-on" strategy.

Personalized Anniversary Promotions

Stephen Fossler built a successful and constantly growing business by learning three things about companies: the company's name and address, the owner or president's full name, and the date the company was founded. Fossler knew that every five years a company reaches a "milestone." What was his idea? "I can help them announce their success and the strength of their companies with Personalized Anniversary Promotions."

Carefully timed mailings reach prospects and customers as they approach their next milestone:

> "**Congratulations on your 15th Business Anniversary this year!** You've accomplished something very special. Many companies never make it to their milestone Anniversary like you have." His original promotion was an Anniversary Foil Seal, recognized the world over as the traditional symbol of business success.

Anniversary Foil Seals contain the company name and the business anniversary milestone. They come in a variety of designs and colors and are easy to use all year long as an elegant, subtle reminder of the company's success. Seals are placed on everything from letterheads and invoices to brochures, catalogs, envelopes, gift certificates, purchase orders, warranties and products.

Fossler's promotion ideas were later expanded to include more than 124 promotion ideas included in a free, *Fossler's Guide to Planning & Promoting Your Business Anniversary.*

The business generated by his Anniversary Foil Seals idea paid off for Fossler on January 7, 2004: New England Business Service, a business forms and packaging supplies marketer acquired Stephen Fossler Company for $27 million cash.

Brainstorming sessions generate lots of good ideas.

Perhaps you're familiar with *brainstorming* – it's an idea generating process. It's easy and fun to do. By yourself, make notes with pad and pencil. In a group, encourage others to join in. Or, try brainstorming with the help of computer software.

Follow these easy-to-follow brainstorming rules: Organize information — create outlines, charts, flashcards, timelines, and concept maps to help visualize relationships. Try to integrate what you're looking for with what you already know.

Enforce this rule: No idea is a *bad* idea. Think creatively. Don't be afraid to take risks. No criticism allowed! List all the ideas. Then, review the ideas. Trim the list to the best 5 ideas. Check each for requirements or restrictions.

If you start losing focus, take a break! Switch the type of task you're working on, the subject you're examining, or the environment you're in. Stop the session when you're no longer being productive.

The Focus Funnel helps select your winning Idea Value Driver:

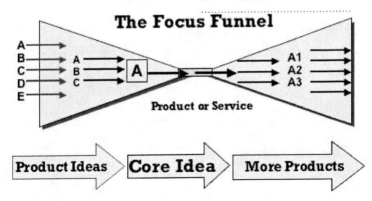

Core Idea Development

The Focus Funnel

Product or Service

Product Ideas → Core Idea → More Products

Start at the left to use the Focus Funnel: List your 5 ideas. Of the 5 best ideas, which three ideas do you *think* will have more meaning to customers?

Examine each idea carefully for its potential. Weed down to 3 ideas. Repeat the process until you select one idea – **"A"** – as your **Value Driver Idea**.

Later on you can look for **Extensions** with closely related products or services (P1, P2 and P3) Extensions lead to even more expansion, as each product proves successful. For example, a dry cleaning store *extends* their core service by offering dress shirt laundry or fur storage.

Find data to evaluate your winning idea. Search the Internet. When hard data isn't available, try to be simpleminded. Rely on common sense. *Think like a customer!* What would be in the customer's best interests? Talk to customers. Listen.

Be obsessive in your thinking! But be flexible! If you pound your head against the wall, you'll never see a different solution to the problem you're trying to solve.

Be stubborn, have courage – don't give up on our idea too soon. What are the most obvious reasons for acceptance... or rejection? Why will some folks accept your idea? Or others reject it out-of-hand?

Years ago, Walt Disney said wistfully, "I only hope that we don't lose sight of one thing – that it was all started by a mouse."

Disney recognized the principle of selecting the best idea and told his people, "Get a good idea and stay with it. Dog it, and work at it until it's done right."

The problem is how to select the *right* idea when there are many on the table. A valid Idea Value Driver responds clearly with one clear statement: THIS is what I DO that has value to my customers!

A Case Story: Ivory Soap

No one knows who discovered soap – but this tale *could* be true!

In Caesar's times there were crude altars outside Rome on Sapo Hill where the poor made sacrifices to their gods. They burned sacrificial animals on these altars. Fat rendered from the animals accumulated on the altars, and so did ash. Rain fell, leaching alkali from the ash and carried the fat and alkali down through the heavy clay soil.

Soon, women learned this soapy clay made washing clothes easier. Sapo clay, some say, was the origin of soap. A derivative of Sapo is found in the word for soap in many European languages – soap, sapone, savon, jabon, seife.

Whether you believe this tale or not, it's likely that soap was discovered by boiling tallow (fat of certain animals) and wood ashes together. To make soap in the home, a woman collected fat drippings in a kettle on the back of the stove. Then she poured hot water through wood ashes to get potash. When she boiled fat and potash together, the result was a harsh, strong yellow soap. Cut into bars, yellow soap was used for both washing clothes and bathing – it was harsh on skin and hands.

The early American commercial soap makers – such as Procter & Gamble, founded in 1837 – made their yellow soap outdoors in great iron kettles, but used a standard formula to insure somewhat better quality. Their soap wasn't quite as harsh as the homemade variety.

James Gamble & Harley Procter – focus on changing a commodity market!

During the 1870's, two partners, James Gamble and Harley Procter, envisioned how they could create an exciting and profitable change in the yellow soap market, a well-established commodity market.

This is how their Idea Value Driver *might* have read...

> **What can we DO for the customer?**
>
> IF we create a *white* bar soap that's ideal for *both* bathing and washing clothes – gentle on skin and hands and gets clothes clean – THEN folks will prefer buying our soap!

In 1878, after years of experimentation with various formulations, Gamble triumphantly reported that they had developed the formula and process for a *white soap* that was "satisfactory in every respect".

At first, the product was to be called P&G White Soap. But Harley Procter insisted the new white soap deserved a more *distinctive* name – one which people would remember when they went to the store.

Procter had a sudden flash of inspiration while attending Sunday church service. The search for a name ended when the minister read from Psalms 45:8, *"All thy garments smell of myrrh and aloes and cassia, out of the ivory palaces whereby they have made thee glad."*

During October 1879, the first bar of Ivory Soap was sold. And, as the business developed, more values were added to their original idea...

Ivory Soap, It Floats! Ivory's most famous feature—its ability to float—*was the result of an accident!* An employee failed to shut off the soap-making machine when he went to lunch. When he returned, he found the soap mixture puffed-up and frothy. After consulting with his supervisor, the decision was made to finish and ship the soap since the ingredients hadn't been changed by the longer mixing time.

About a month later, P&G received orders for more of "that floating soap." The people in the Order Department were perplexed. Only after some detective work was the mystery solved. The long forgotten lunchtime accident *had produced a floating soap!*

Since then, Ivory floats because P&G intentionally whips a small amount of air into Ivory as it's being made. This makes the soap lighter than water, so it floats. That means it's easier to find in the bath or washtub. It also makes each bar of Ivory velvety smooth and easy to lather.

99 - 44/100% PURE® - This famous slogan originated when Harley Procter sent samples of Ivory to college chemistry professors and independent laboratories for analysis. Comparison tests were made with castile soaps—the standard of excellence at that time.

One chemist's analysis was in table form with the ingredients listed by percentage. Procter totaled the ingredients that did not fall into the category of pure soap—they equaled 56/100%. He subtracted from 100, and wrote the slogan "99-44/100% Pure®" This became a pledge of quality to Ivory consumers.

So let's update Harley Procter & James Gamble's original Idea Value Driver...

Ivory Soap, 1879 – Replace Yellow Soaps

Value Driver Idea –What do we DO for the customer?

Ivory Soap — a *white* bar soap—is ideal for bathing and washing clothes. Ivory is mild and gentle on skin and hands, powerful on dirt...and it floats! Ivory is 99-44/100% Pure®

And folks did prefer buying their soap! Ivory replaced old-fashioned yellow soaps and added new customers from the higher priced castile soap market.

Washing machines came into homes in the early 1900's. That's when P&G learned that homemakers cut off slivers of laundry soap for washing clothes so the soap would dissolve faster in their washing machines. So P&G began doing this for them by marketing soap flakes, Ivory Flakes.

While soaps have remained as popular for personal use, their use for general laundering and dish washing decreased after WW II. Consumers replaced soap with synthetic detergents because of their lower cost and their greater efficiency.

Tide, P&G's leading detergent brand, was launched in a test market in 1946. By 1949, it had expanded nationally. The first advertising theme, "Cleaner than any soap," was replaced in 1949 with "Tide's in, Dirt's out". Tide achieved market leadership three months after going national and has never lost that leadership.

125 Years later, Ivory is still a major P&G brand.

The original Idea Value Driver – mild and gentle on skin and hands, powerful on dirt – is as good today as it was in 1879. Ivory's Extensions have been updated to meet a constantly changing and expanding marketplace…

The **Classic Ivory** 99 44/100% Pure Floating Soap cleanses the skin by removing dirt and oils that can clog pores. It contains no heavy perfumes, creams, or dyes.

Ivory Hand Soap - A mild, liquid hand cleanser —with the convenience of a pump—washes away bacteria, yet gentle enough even for your face.

Ivory Body Wash - With pure and mild cleansers, gives you rich and creamy moisturizing lather, leaving your skin feeling surprisingly smooth and unmistakably baby soft.

Ivory Liqui-Gel - A mild, liquid hand cleanser washes away dirt and bacteria, yet is gentle enough even for your face.

Ivory Snow — For over 60 years mothers trusted Ivory Snow® to care for their baby's garments. Great for your washable wools, silks and cottons.

Value Driver IDEA Summary:

What it is you do is defined from the Customer's point-of-view. The idea selector format stimulates clear thinking when developing new business ideas. Take time to listen to your customers. Learn about your customers and prospects. Brainstorming sessions generate good ideas and build an idea inventory. The Focus Funnel helps select *the* Core Idea. Daring to be different can build a business others may take years trying to copy. But a good idea can hook on to other's success. One idea can change a well-established price driven commodity market.

Task N° 1 – The Idea

Now, let's get started. Go to your **Core Value Proposition Worksheet**, please set up your business building Idea.

Idea –What do we DO for the customer?	

| Value Driver Benefit | How does the Customer benefit from your Idea? |

"No man can withstand the strength of an idea whose time has come."- Victor Hugo

Let's talk about Features, Benefits ...and Advantages!

Features define a product or a service. They are what a product or service _IS. Features consist of *physical* characteristics, such as color, size, smell, weight, and material composition. They also consist of *functional* characteristics, such as speed, duration, power, frequency, applicability, effectiveness, and availability.

Benefits flow from the features of a product or service. They are what a product or service *does* for the customer.

Advantages are the result of comparing competitive features and/or benefits of a product or service.

DANGER: Take care not to confuse features, benefits and advantages. In trouble-free terms, a person buys a product because of its benefits, not only because of its features. Features are what a product or service is. Benefits are the *"what it does for me."* Advantages become evident when products or services *are compared.* This one is better than the other.

Benefits help you thrive in a price dominated market!

There is an inverse relationship between the Customer's perception of benefits and price: As the number of benefits increase, price has less importance.

- In a **value driven market**, perceived benefits are the principal drivers – *price has little or no effect.*

- In a **commodity market**, there are no a perceived benefits *price is the single, solitary driver.*

How can you thrive? If you've got any doubts, tap into your innovative capabilities: ignore most conventional knowledge, disregard a consultant's "wisdom", forget standards and benchmarks. *Create a difference!*

Innovation: "POD" changes traditional book publishing

Traditional royalty book publishing is a well-established business model. The publisher screens authors and books for quality and marketability. Then, at their own cost, the publisher manages editing, manufacturing, marketing, promotion, sales, warehousing, and fulfillment.

The author receives a percentage royalty on sales. The costs involved in royalty book publishing are extremely high. And, the number of authors whom eventually succeed in publishing their works is disproportionately low.

In the past, some authors – disheartened by the traditional business model – published and marketed their own works It's called "vanity" publishing. Authors could expect a minimum order of 5,000 copies and publishing costs of $20,000. Add to that marketing expenses and inventory storage. The "vanity" publishing process could take months.

New printing technology emerged during 1994 creating a change in the book publishing industry's model. It's called Printing-On-Demand. POD publishing is a practical combination of conventional publishing tasks, just-in-time manufacturing and Internet marketing and retailing.

Authors and writers prepare their works for publication. Their tools include Microsoft's Word, QuarkExpress, Adobe's Pagemaker or InDesign and Acrobat PDF. Learning to use these tools is easy, costs are low and results can be highly rewarding.

The new printing POD publisher provides fast service. Books are ready to be published within 4 to 6 weeks after receiving the author's manuscript.

POD books are stored digitally. As orders are received, the POD publisher prints just the number ordered. Delivery? Books are printed, bound and shipped within 3 to 6 days of receiving each customer order. And, POD publishers offer marketing support from their own online bookstores as well as listing with some of the world's most visited on-line and traditional bookstores.

As a result, authors don't need to hesitate thinking about publishing their works. No book need ever be out-dated, out-of-print or back-ordered. POD manufacturing means no inventory investment for preprinted books. And, no waste from unwanted or outdated books.

Check out some of POD's benefits and advantages...

POD Publishing Benefits:
Benefits: What's in it for the author?

Affordable startup cost (under $1,000). Publisher handles legal and administrative requirements; helps with publicity and manages retail sales. Author retains copyright, sets retail price, decides on design and appearance, and directs publicity work. No minimum volume requirement. Author also sells direct to customer.

Advantages: Fast publication (4 to 6 weeks); Improved income potential. No inventory storage. Instant content updates with minimal cost.

• • •

A Core Value Proposition revolutionized the airline industry!

Case Story: Southwest Airlines

"Southwest Airlines: The Hottest Thing in the Sky"

FORTUNE Magazine, March 8, 2004 issue reported... "It's a little strange how some folks still think about the airline business. There are the big players, they'll tell you, like Delta, United, and American. And then you have the smaller fish. The low-cost carriers, led by that wacky Southwest Airlines, which they mention almost as an afterthought."

Southwest Airlines: In 2003 the company earned $442 million—more than all the other U.S. airlines combined. Its market capitalization of $11.7 billion was bigger than that of all its competitors combined, too. And in May 2004, according to the Department of Transportation, Southwest boarded more domestic customers than any other airline.

Sure, the "traditionals" have more revenue—Southwest ranks only N° 7 with about $6 billion in sales in 2003. And the traditional airlines have more planes and carry more passengers *when you include their overseas routes.*

But look at a key metric used in the airline business: cost per available seat mile (CASM). In 1995 Southwest's CASM was 7.07 cents. In 2004 it is up to 7.60 cents. The traditional airlines all have CASMs of between 9 cents and 13 cents. Of course, some analysts question whether Southwest's outstanding growth trajectory can continue.

The bottom line reads loud and clear!

How did Southwest get there? We've got to go back to the airline's conception. Southwest began 33 years ago when Herb Kelleher (a lawyer by training) and a partner wrote the beginnings of a business plan on a cocktail napkin. They saw opportunity in the faults of the hub-and-spoke model used by traditional carriers. They also recognized customers were turned off by airline employees with an "I don't care" attitude.

What can we DO for the customer?

Some say Kelleher's idea read like this...

> "**IF** we get our passengers to their destinations when they want to get there, on time, at the lowest possible fares, and make darn sure they have a good time doing it, **THEN** people will fly our airline."

Over the years, Southwest has kept Core Value Idea intact.

Southwest's Idea Value Driver concentrates upon **three customer benefits**:

- On time, convenient departures and arrivals;
- Lowest possible fares; and,
- A good time getting there.

In practice, two more benefits were identified:

- Faster travel, door-to-door;
- Safe aircraft.

Texas is a big state. When Southwest started operations, many frequent city-to-city travelers drove rather than fly. The hub-and-spoke model airlines used was not customer friendly...few if any direct flights. Driving city-to-city could be faster and less bothering.

Southwest flies city-to-city. They want no part of the hub-and-spoke model. They enter markets in which traditional airlines control market share. They hit competition with much lower fares to attract new customers. The positive travel experience keeps customers coming back.

Results? In the early '90s, Southwest entered Baltimore Washington International Airport (BWI). US Air had a significant BWI hub. Southwest took No. 1 of traffic at BWI with a 47% share. US Air went down to 4.9% share.

Much to many traditional airlines surprise, Southwest flies *only* 737s. That makes crew training and aircraft service and maintenance easier, faster and cost efficient. Their aircraft turnaround time is 29 minutes (get ready time needed for next departure). The competition? *Almost twice that!*

Southwest serves no meals, only the usual snacks. They charge no fees to change same-fare tickets. And there are no assigned seats. They fly from and to less crowded airports. They have no electronic entertainment on its planes. Instead, fun flight attendants relentlessly amuse passengers.

Colleen Barrett, Southwest's President and Chief Operating Officer told reporters, "We were the first airline to win the coveted Triple Crown for a month - Best On-time Record, Best Baggage Handling, and Fewest Customer Complaints. Since then we've won it more than thirty times, as well as five annual Triple Crowns for 1992, 1993, 1994, 1995, and 1996."

She went on to say, "We were the first airline with a frequent flyer program to give credit for the <u>number of trips taken</u> and not the number of miles flown." "We pioneered unique programs: Senior Discounts, Fun Fares, Fun Packs, a same-day air freight delivery service, no ticket travel, and many others"

In fact, Herb Kelleher "hard wired" his organization's thinking on innovation right from the start. Any innovation that drives the cost structure down or that passengers are willing to pay for is welcome aboard!

So far, Southwest's Value Driven Idea has proven unbeatable. It provides a central focus to all facets of the airline's operations. Let's see how Southwest Airlines' Idea Value Driver and its Benefits fit into our Core Value analysis:

Southwest Airlines Value Drivers

Idea - Frequent direct flights, city-to-city; distance, 150-300 miles.

Benefits - Go when I want to go! On time, frequent and convenient departures and arrivals. Lowest possible fares. Safe new aircraft. A good time getting there. Plus advantages: Faster travel, door-to-door; less expensive than driving; less crowded airports.

Target - Mostly business people making frequent trips city-to-city, folks who stay in destination, who give value to saving travel time.

Perception - I get to my destination when I want to, on time, with the lowest possible fare and have a good time doing it.

Reward - A profitable airline – a fun place to work.

How did customers react to Southwest's Values?

Several customers commented: "Saves me significant travel time, door-to-door." "Sure makes flying fun." "Saves me money."

Value Driver BENEFIT Summary:

The Customer must benefit from your Idea. And they must be benefits and advantages that are important. Benefits coming from new technology can change an industry overnight. If you use benefits wisely, you can thrive in a "dismal" market dominated by price! Learn to apply the inverse relationship between the customer's perception of benefits and price. One 38 word, benefit-driven idea revolutionized the entire airline industry!

Task N° 2 – Benefits

Now it's time for your next task: Go to your **Core Value Proposition Worksheet**. Please put together your Idea's business building Benefits.

Benefits – What's in it for the customer? Compared to competition?	

Use this Benefit Value Driver Checklist

☐ **Think like a customer!** Listen to your customers. Have you experienced first-hand how your benefits fit into the Customer's life? Can you develop an even greater perceived or real benefit differentiation?

☐ **Or, should you think like Amazon's Jeff Bezos?** Constantly introduce small but innovative features and benefits that add up to a *superlative* experience for customers.

☐ **Will your benefits really deliver a superior value?** Do you believe customers will agree that the new benefit value is superior to the competition? How much money will you save the customer? Or, how much will employee productivity be increased?

☐ **Can you sustain both benefits and advantages over time?** Will you have proprietary technology? Or will you need to create other barriers to competitive entry? Are you confident your organization can create and sustain the needed capabilities to put your Value Driver's promise into operation?

☐ **Last but not least: Make a comparison!** Compare your Value Driver benefits to the competition. Make a comparative list to be sure of each point of differentiation – features, benefits and advantages.

It's worth a double check!

"There's always an opportunity to make a difference."
— Michael Dell

How can they be identified?
How can they be reached?

Think of a target! The bull's eye is small but always represents the highest value. The ring just outside of the bull's eye is a bit larger, easier to hit but not as valuable. The next ring is even larger, but has lots less value. Hit outside the target? No value at all! Defining your Target concentrates business development on one or a just a few key market segments. This is the foundation of effective marketing.

How do you identify market segments most likely to become your customer? Here are *two* frequently used starting points:

1. Geographic Influence – Focus upon serving the needs of customers in a specific geographical area. Identify the "where"; and,

2. Socio-Cultural Influence -- Think about "clusters." It's said, "birds of a feather flock together!" Companies do it. People do it too! Identify groups of people most likely to buy your product or service. Focus upon potential heavy users before trying to develop new uses.

When you keep product benefits in mind, it's possible to identify specific groups – each with different motives or life styles – that could view your product or service values to be important. As you identify characteristics of potential customers, you begin a market segmentation process.

Segmentation divides the market into classes or categories of people or firms based upon a distinctive set of factors. It allows identification of *where* potential customers are and *how many* there are. As market segmentation continues, what at first appeared blurred begins to develop into clearly defined target groups. Identifying each group leads to an effective marketing strategy.

JCPenney has approximately 1,075 department stores in all 50 U.S. states, Puerto Rico, and Mexico. Each store serves a local market.

JCPenney targets their customers with a life style selector: "Our target - customer segments - are **'Modern Spenders'** and **'Starting Outs,'** who shop for apparel, accessories, and home furnishings in the shopping centers where JCPenney is located."

The Modern Spenders are mostly dual-earner households with up to two children...consumption oriented. **The Starting Outs** are typically single or a young family with up to one child...establishing their shopping patterns. **Median annual household income: $48,000. Plus: Multi-cultural customers** within target segments.

These targeting criteria are found within commercial research studies and databases. They provide a Penney with focus that extends to store design, merchandise selection, merchandising, advertising and promotion.

• • •

Two *indestructible* business rules apply to targeting... (see Post Data)

Rule 2: The more you know about your Customer, the more likely it is you can offer the *right* product, at the *right* time, in the *right* place with the *right* price.

Rule 3: Customers are the best and least expensive source of new or additional sales.

A classic Barbershop story...

Years ago I moved to Rio de Janeiro, Brazil. I had to find a barber. It should be easy but it's always a chore. My friend, Antonio, suggested I might try his barbershop in downtown Rio, just a short drive from my office.

I copied his directions: "Reinaldo's Barbershop, on the fourth floor of second office building just off Avenida Rio Branco. There's a small red and white barber's pole near the building's entrance." Antonio added, "Reinaldo is a great barber but he really needs marketing help!"

I spotted the building, took the elevator to the fourth floor. I found Reinaldo's Barber Shop a few steps down the hall. The shop had six chairs but Reinaldo was the only barber.

Reinaldo told me, "In better days I had four others working with me. But I let the last one go two weeks ago. Not enough business!" So I got my hair cut. It was a good one, just as I like.

And we talked about his business. He was in the center of Rio's main business district – a good location even if it was somewhat difficult to find. I asked Reinaldo if he had a client list. "No, but I can put one together." We talked about differences in customer's haircut frequency. We set up a classification for customers: A, B, C and D.

It's amazing how many businesses fail to establish and use this customer information.

"A" folks come in every week, their appearance is important –TV personalities, important politicians and bankers. **"B"** people come in every 2 to 3 weeks; **"C"** every 3 to 4 weeks. And, **"D"** folks (like me), come in when they see themselves in the mirror and say, "I've got to get a haircut this week! (4 to 6 weeks).

Rule 2 kicked in: The more you know about your Customer, the more likely it is you can offer the right product, at the right time, in the right place with the right price.

Reinaldo put together a client list, and added classification criteria – picked up telephone numbers addresses, secretary's name. We added several other items needed to remember and communicate with each client.

By the way, Reinaldo didn't have a computer. All this was done with an address book and an agenda. As customers came in, Reinaldo would discreetly verify preferences. "Do you prefer Tuesdays in the morning?" He tentatively scheduled the next appointment using his classification criteria.

Then Reinaldo began calling his customers to confirm their next appointment. He'd speak with the secretary, "Please ask Mr. Motta if he prefers 10 or 10:30 next Tuesday morning." That technique encouraged "B", "C" and "D" customers to come in more frequently than they would *without* a reminder.

Do the numbers – Coming in more frequently meant more income! Convert a "D" customer (10 haircuts a year) to a "C" customer (17 a year) and Reinaldo got 7 more haircuts from the same customer.

Much to his surprise, customers reacted very positively to his calls confirming appointments. Other barbershops followed the walk-in and wait tradition. Reinaldo's appointments were considered a point of prestige…and saved valuable executive time.

Then Rule 3 came into play: Customers are the best and least expensive source of new or additional sales volume. Reinaldo's appointment technique encouraged customers to talk about his service, give referrals. *And they did!*

A long story short: Reinaldo followed Walt Disney's advice, "Get a good idea and stay with it. Dog it, and work at it until it's done right." Reinaldo kept perfecting the system. Six months later two barbers were back in the shop. One year later all six chairs were busy. An assistant was handling the telephone, agenda and address book.

• • •

A fast growing brand in the world's oldest category!
Case Story: King Arthur Baking Flour

Here's a unique Case Story demonstrating the business development power of an intelligent, precise targeting strategy plus a corporate culture rarely found…

During 2003 while baking flour market leaders – Gold Medal and Pillsbury – saw their volume *go down* as the market shrank. The impact of carbohydrate conscious diets resulted in less in home baking.

But King Arthur Flour had a 20% sales growth! Sales of over $35 million. King Arthur is now N°3 in the market and growing fast. Their Whole Wheat Flour is already N° 1!

How did they do it? It's a great Case Story – one where targeting played a major role. *So, here's the rest of the story!* '

The Sands, Taylor and Wood Co. began operation in 1790. That makes King Arthur the oldest flour company in America. The company was headquartered on Boston's Long Wharf and imported quality flour from England. Since it's beginning King Arthur sells only unbleached, un-bromated milled flour with absolutely no chemical additives. A high protein, quality flour that has earned rave reviews from bakery chefs worldwide.

In 1896, its three owners were stumped. They were rolling out a new flour brand, but were couldn't decide on a name. George Wood, one of the company's founders, came up with the name, King Arthur Flour. Woods felt the ideals of King Arthur matched the attributes of their new flour perfectly: strength (high protein) and purity (no chemical additives). The name King Arthur proved so powerful it eventually stood for the company itself.

In 1984 King Arthur Flour moved to the scenic Connecticut River valley town of Norwich, Vermont just across the river from Hanover, New Hampshire.

Early on in the 1990's management was looking for a new approach to restructure their company. So they looked to the legend of King Arthur's Round Table for inspiration. It seemed only natural to structure the company the same way King Arthur did with his knights. In 1996, an Employee Stock Ownership Plan was launched putting ownership of The King Arthur Flour Company in the hands of its employees. King Arthur Flour Company has over 160 owners. Like their predecessors of 1896, King Arthur folks want their products and corporate life to express the integrity, strength, reliability, and superior performance. A team built on firm principles and a group effort.

When talking about themselves and their business culture, they say...

We define ourselves as "A Threshold Company"

Harvard Business Review defines a threshold company as one that outpaces its larger competitors, outpaces the industry, and outpaces the economy. King Arthur Flour management says, "We are on the threshold of bigness."

Four themes run through King Arthur's culture

"First, we have an earned respect. There is a sense that our enterprise is special in what it stands for, what it does, and how we do it. As such we deserve and expect uncommon effort and contribution from those who work here and those with whom we work."

"Second, we have an almost evangelical zeal — an honest enthusiasm that spills over onto those with whom we do business, from current and prospective employees, to customers, and suppliers."

"**Third, we have a habit of dealing people in** — we communicate just about everything to everybody in our organization and we empower them as partners in our crusade. Strategies, plans, ambitions, and problems are not the secrets of the 'palace guard' – they are known and appreciated throughout our company."

"**Fourth, we view profit and wealth-creation as inevitable byproducts** of doing things well. Making money as an end in itself is not our highest priority."

The result is a corporate culture of incredible passion and sincerity. One that compels them to honor their customers and honor a company they all can truly call their own. Some may scoff at such high ideals in today's business world. But to a member of the Round Table, there is no other way to successfully run a company.

How does targeting fit into King Arthur's business building plans?

King Arthur's Target Value Driver

King Arthur's focus is upon professional bakers and serious baking hobbyists. These are folks deeply involved with baking, heavy users who can influence brand preference and purchase. King Arthur reaches out to these folks through multiple communication and distribution channels.

The Baker's Catalogue: The company's commitment to bringing back the American tradition of home baking, provided the incentive for the introduction of *The Baker's Catalogue*® in 1990. Since then, the catalogue has grown in leaps and bounds, reaching baking enthusiasts around the world. The Baker's Catalogue® offers professional quality baking equipment and ingredients, including whole grains, hard-to-find specialty flours, dried fruits, chocolates and a full line of signature King Arthur® Flour baking mixes.

In 1990, 250,000 black & white digest-size catalogues were mailed to approximately 250,000 households – in 2004, 7 million 56-page full-color, full-size catalogues were mailed to baking enthusiasts.

The Baker's Retail Store: In October of 1992, the company opened **The Baker's Store**, an interactive version of the catalogue, located on Route 5 South in Norwich, Vermont. The in-store test kitchen is staffed daily with experienced bakers eager to answer customer's questions while demonstrating some of their favorite products and baking techniques. The shelves are stocked with all the wares featured in the catalogue as well as local products and Vermont-made specialties.

In 1993, the store was 144 square feet in size, with gross sales of $48,000. Today The Baker's Store is 2,100 square feet in size, with gross sales of over $2,000,000. Approximately 50% of the store's customers come from states other than Vermont or New Hampshire.

Today, visitors to Norwich can shop, take classes, enjoy over 600 recipes, study King Arthur's history, find out where King Arthur® Flour is available, read about upcoming events at The Baker's Store, and check out the course schedule for The Baking Education Center.

Professional Education: The recent addition of **The Baking Education Center** in Norwich helps the company continue its commitment to education through an extensive curriculum of demonstration, lecture-style and hands-on courses. The school welcomes all bakers, from beginner to professional.

King Arthur's Professional Bakers travel the country presenting free baking classes for adults. For over 20 years they've shared the secrets to successful baking at classes held in supermarkets, community clubs, banquet rooms and church halls, teaching thousands of people around the country.

In January of 1992 the company introduced the **Life Skills Bread Baking Program®** to introduce the joy of baking to youngsters. The program is geared towards middle school students and teaches basic baking skills through demonstrations presented by King Arthur® instructors.

Internet: www.KingArthurFlour.com – In August of 1997, King Arthur's website was unveiled with the goal of providing customers information about the company and its products. The site quickly grew to include online baking classes and has become a treasure trove of recipes. In late 1999 The **Baker's Catalogue®** was added to the website, making it fully e-commerce oriented and enhancing its value as a baking resource.

The online Baking Circle is an active group of more than 100,000 members all with a keen interest in baking. As a forum, members ask and answer baking questions, share personal recipes, and hear the advice of fellow bakers. For King Arthur it is an invaluable compendium of past messages that serve as an ever-increasing archive of baking information.

Supermarkets in all 50 States: In 1993, King Arthur Flour was sold in just 11 states. Today King Arthur Flour is found in all 50 states. It is the number-one selling flour in New England, and the number-one selling unbleached flour in every market where they have full distribution. Loyal King Arthur consumers, serious baking hobbyists, are the driving force gaining distribution against competitive pressures and formidable buyer resistance.

From this dynamic marketing background, five Value Drivers and a Value Proposition can be identified and defined for King Arthur Flour...

Core Value Proposition

King Arthur® Flour Value Drivers

Idea –What do we DO for the customer?

Provide excellent baking results. We are dedicated to bringing back the American tradition of home baking. Our milled flour, unbleached and un-bromated, has high protein content, no chemical additives and is celebrated by bakery chefs, worldwide.

Benefits – What's in it for the customer? Compared to competition?

We are a source of valuable recipes and learning new baking techniques. Interaction with others involved in baking as a hobby and profession. A source of difficult to find baking products; a full array of corollary baking products and educational services.

Target – Who is in the Target Market? How identified separately from others?

Our primary target includes professional bakers and serious baking hobbyists. Folks who are deeply involved with baking. Heavy users who can influence brand preference and purchase. We reach out to these folks through several communication and distribution channels.

Perception – How do WE want to be perceived?

We have an almost evangelical zeal – an honest enthusiasm that spills over onto those with whom we do business, from our customers and suppliers to current and prospective employees. Our enterprise is special in what it stands for, what it does, and how we do it. As such we deserve and expect uncommon effort and contribution from those who work here and those with whom we work.

Reward – What's in it for us?

We view profit and wealth-creation as inevitable byproducts of doing things well and enjoying what we do.

Core Value Proposition

We are a flourmill dedicated to bringing back the American tradition of home baking through close contact with professional bakers and serious baking hobbyists. We meet our challenge with a corporate culture of incredible passion and sincerity. One that compels us to honor our customers and celebrate a company all our people can truly call their own.

Value Driver TARGET Summary:

Who is in your target market? How do you reach them? Take time to find and identify market segments most likely to become your customer. Use two durable targeting rules: Customers are the best and least expensive source of new or additional sales. And, the more you know about your Customer, the more likely it is you can offer the right product, at the right time, at the right place with the right price. When their market shrank, the two market leaders volume went down – but the third place brand – using smart targeting – generated a 20% sales growth.

Task N° 3 – Target

It's time to identify your Idea's Target. Go to your **Core Value Proposition Worksheet.** Please define your Target. Use the checklist as a aid.

Target – Who is in the Target market? How can they be identified separately from others?	

Targeting Checklist

☐ **Define and redefine** your target market, your audience. Identify sub-sections. Sub-sections? Think about "clusters." It's said, "birds of a feather flock together!" Companies do it. People do it. You saw how King Arthur identified their clusters: professional bakers and serious baking hobbyists.

☐ **How would you group your present customers?** Is this grouping compatible with your idea? If not, what new groups have to be added? Deleted? Search and study your present and past customer transactions. Find both the good and the bad. How does each reflect upon your target selection

☐ **Remember, business and consumer marketing are different.** In either one you will want to identify and understand the people who are involved.

☐ **Pay attention to individual perspectives** and needs of each customer as you define your target. Match that against your Idea and Benefits. Does it fit? If not, why?

☐ **Are you sure you have enough potential customers** in your target to *really* make up a viable market in terms of revenue?

☐ **There is no such thing as a mass market.** Targets are made up of individuals. And, effective communications are written from one person to another. When a target is defined in the millions, it rarely reaches anyone.

┌──────────────────────────────┬──────────────────────────────┐
| **Value Driver** | How do you want |
| **Perception** | to be perceived? |
└──────────────────────────────┴──────────────────────────────┘

"There is no better exercise for the heart
than reaching out and lifting people up." – Unknown

Perception is an attitude or understanding based upon
what we observe or think or do.

We unconsciously develop perceptions about companies
and people. We're influenced in building our perceptions by a
wide-range of information: Internet, TV, radio and magazine
advertising, news reports and friends, others who use a
product or service.

Perception is based not on logic, but on experience – the
combination of both logic and emotion. The *critical influence*
that gives final form to our perception is the experience when
we *use* a product and service.

One purpose of this chapter is to help you learn to think
like a customer.

Thinking like a customer compels us to become one of our
target customers. We take a critical glimpse at ourselves
looking in from the outside *rather than from the inside looking out.*
With a customer's perspective, we can gain a better
understanding of the customer's anticipated experience with
our product or service.

A clear statement – how *you want your customers to perceive your
product of service* – establishes guidelines for a business model
and your organization structure.

Here are two case stories that provide an insight to customer perceptions. Both these companies are built upon powerful ideas and benefits, both are leaders in their markets...

Case Story: Cobalt Boats

Have you ever *owned* a boat? Or *dreamed* about owning a boat? I've done both! When I opened Cobalt Boats newest brochure, this message *really* hit home...

> **"Who can say when first you heard?** The multicolored minute when the·open water spoke, and the dream began. *Try now.* To this day, can you recall the moment? Can you reach back and listen again to that faint, this green-flecked whisper – *relentless as a mother's summons* – coming from just beyond the farthest thing a kid could ever hope to see. Our name is Cobalt. *We build boats that answer the call."*

I said to myself, "Jack, you have to learn more about Cobalt Boats!" Soon after, the August 2004 issue of *Inc. magazine* arrived in my mailbox. That's where I learned Cobalt's remarkable story...*the headline declared...*

The unlikely story of Cobalt Boats

"At the big-city winter boat shows, the crowds thicken near the 20 to 36-foot, $30,000 to $300,000 runabouts made by Cobalt Boats. They're beautiful crafts, recognizable from afar by their sleek lines and flowing power humps, and show visitors often ask where the boats are made. The answer can startle them."

"Cobalt boats, widely admired as the Steinways of the runabout class – roughly defined as "trailerable" craft with inboard motors – are built about as far from a lapping tide as is geographically possible in America. Future owners who desire a peek at their boat under construction, as some do, drive through rolling prairie land dotted with cattle and blanketed with fields of milo, alfalfa, and wheat. It's all humming highway until you slow for the one-stoplight town of Neodesha (pronounced Nee-oh-de-shay), Kansas (population, 2,800). This is Cobalt's home."

"If building high-performance boats in the heart of the prairie seems unlikely, consider that most of the people making them are classic landlubbers, *farmers* to the core. These second- and third-generation farmers, some of them still working their land, many of them still stinging from their loss of it, are Cobalt's unique competitive advantage."

Company founder Pack St. Clair doesn't remember exactly when, but at some point early in the company's history it dawned on him: Most of the employees he valued most came to work wearing cowboy boots and big belt buckles. "I didn't go looking for farmers," St. Clair recalls, "but I found out they were the ones who worked hardest."

JD Power Award for Customer Satisfaction:

The proof of those qualities is the company's lock on a JD Power award for customer satisfaction. Last year, as in two previous years, Cobalt finished first among builders of 20- to 29-foot runabouts…far ahead of the runner-up. Download the latest brochure at www.cobaltboats.com. Market share is up nearly a percentage point, to nearly 5%. The largest competitor, Sea Ray, commands just 12% of the family runabout market.

So with Cobalt's information at hand, I put together a ...

Cobalt Perception Value Driver:

> Cobalt Boats aspire to a single objective: Water bound fun for family and friends. We design and manufacture an unbroken succession of boats that make the best use of technology, boats that incorporate imagination and innovation in ever-new iterations of nautical science. Cobalt Boats represent an uncommon value. Value born of an insistence upon the ultimate importance of details. Details, when seen even from afar, gather toward greatness.

That's how customers, prospects and their own people perceive Cobalt Boats.

Case Story - J.M. Smucker

Here's another case with an equally vibrant background – *another* company in business for over 100 years. But now facing the challenge of expanding its perception to other, recently acquired product lines.

"With a name like Smucker's, it has to be good!"

Smucker's likes to joke about its name. *And it works!* What they're saying is that their name doesn't matter because the product is so good people will buy it instead of others.

The J.M. Smucker Company was founded in 1897 when the Company's namesake and founder sold his first product – apple butter – from the back of a horse-drawn wagon. The company has been family run for four generations and is headquartered in Orrville, Ohio (pop. 8,000), a quiet, tidy town 50 miles south of Cleveland.

It's an over 100-years-old, family-controlled business that is run by two brothers who tend to quote the New Testament and Ben Franklin. It's a throwback to a simpler time. It's said that if Norman Rockwell were to design a corporation, this would be it. In other words, J.M. Smucker & Co. couldn't be trendier.

Smucker was recognized as the top company in *FORTUNE Magazine's* 2003 annual survey of *The 100 Best Companies to Work For.* They've ranked consistently in the top 25 companies each year since *FORTUNE* began the list in 1998.

Management culture starts with their Co-CEOs

Tim and Richard Smucker took the reins in 2001. Tim and Richard are popular with their employees—they're affectionately known as the "boys"—which isn't too surprising given that the company's stock has had a total return of 100% over the past five years. Chances are you have seen them as children walking down a country lane in one of Smucker's TV commercials.

The "boys" engineered Smucker's purchase of Jif and Crisco from Procter & Gamble in 2002. That nearly doubled the company's revenues to $1.3 billion in fiscal 2003. And, on June 18, 2004, they announced the acquisition of International Multifoods Corporation in a transaction valued at $840 million.

The "boys" also make sure Smucker adheres to an extremely simple code of conduct set forth by their father and CEO N° 3, Paul Smucker: Listen with your full attention, look for the good in others, have a sense of humor, and say thank you for a job well done.

Management takes their code of conduct seriously

Plant supervisors have been known to serve barbecues celebrating new production records. Managers routinely thank teams with lunches and gift certificates. There's also the annual commemorative Christmas plate, holiday turkeys, screenings of films in which Smucker's has a tie-in.

Today, Smucker is the market leader in fruit spreads, peanut butter, shortening and oils, ice cream toppings, and health and natural foods beverages in North America under such brands as Smucker's®, Jif® and Crisco®. The International Multifoods Corporation acquisition expands its family of products to include other well-known brands as Pillsbury® baking mixes and ready-to-spread frostings; Hungry Jack® pancake mixes, syrups and potato side dishes, and Martha White® baking mixes and ingredients.

Smucker's Multi-Brand philosophy

Smucker has adopted a multi brand value driven philosophy. Each brand develops its own individual value drivers – as does the original Smucker's line of fruit spreads. As a company, the Smucker name provides a unique tradition and patrimony, one that creates additional value for each brand.

Most likely, the biggest challenge Tim and Richard Smucker have to deal with is to make sure the company's culture stays the way it is. Certainly there are problems as they absorb product acquisitions from P&G and now International Multifoods Corporation. But Smucker's corporate culture should make that task that much easier.

Perception Value Driver: JM Smucker

With a name like Smucker... our products have to be so good that people buy them instead of others. Our traditions, our simple code of conduct guarantees that promise.

Value Driver PERCEPTION Summary:

Perception is based not on logic alone, but on experience – the combination of both logic and emotion. The *critical influence* that gives final form to our perception of a company, its products and services, is the *experience of their use.* Thinking like a customer compels us to become one of our target customers. We see ourselves looking in from the outside *rather than from the inside looking out.* With a customer's perspective, we understand the customer's anticipated experience. A clear statement establishes guidelines for a business model and your organization structure. If you seek a unique value then insist upon the fundamental importance of its details. Details, when seen even from afar, gather toward greatness. Find and nurture a simple code of conduct that brings people together as one.

Task N° 4 – Perception

Now for the fourth task: It's time to identify your Idea's Perception. Go to your **Core Value Proposition Worksheet.** Please state your business building Perception.

Perception - How do WE want to be perceived? By Customers? Employees? Suppliers?	

Value Perception Checklist:

☐ The main element in deciding what business development opportunity to pursue is not what *you* want to give your customers, but what your customers *really want from you.*

☐ When searching for innovative ideas, allow customers to help you make a Wish List.

☐ Your company perception is the result of your customer's experience with your products or service.

☐ Fulfilling that experience expectation is an all-inclusive result of your company's operations. Your business model must be designed to create that perception.

☐ Companies that understand and maintain their core values usually communicate in a way that reflects these values.

"Obstacles are those frightful things you see when you take your eyes off your goal." – Henry Ford

Does the reward meet expectations?

Think about "reward" in two ways. There has to be a financial reward, profit. Without profit, there *is* no business. But, just as important, are the corollary rewards: personal satisfaction, energizing the *right* people, becoming part of the *right* location. This involves how your company works, its business model.

Our objective now is to provide…

Reasonable proof that the idea is financially workable

Be it a company startup or refocus, launch of a new business, creating a new product or service… the Core Value Proposition is developed within the first two steps – now its time to give life to the idea! Prove that it is *financially workable*!

Up until now we've been working to define the Idea, develop its Value Drivers and create the Core Value Proposition. We're certainly *not* ready to do full blown 5-year financials. They may be needed later…*but not now.*

What we need first is reasonable proof that the Core Value Proposition is *financially workable*. We can do that with a condensed Operating Statement or Profit & Loss Statement… let's call it an "educated estimate."

During one of my seminars, a young man looked up and asked, "Jack, just how do you make an 'educated estimate'?" He was obviously concerned when I answered, "I use my trusty crystal ball – it's a good one...works great!"

Six elements provide an "educated estimate"

So I explained: My "educated estimate" uses six major headings from an Operating Statement: Revenue, Cost of Goods, Gross Margin, Marketing Costs, Operating Costs and Income Before Tax.

First, try to estimate, as best you can, what you expect to sell during a year. Think in terms of Units. Now set an average Unit *Selling Price*. Multiply Units by Selling Price and you've got estimated Revenue.

Now, think about the Cost to produce an average Unit during a year. Set an *average* Cost. Then, multiply Units by Cost, and you have Cost of Goods. *Subtract* Cost of Goods from Revenue and you have Gross Margin. Calculate the percentage relation of Gross Margin to Revenue.

Estimate your Marketing and Operating expenses. Be realistic and conservative. Don't try to think Year One, Year Two. Save that detail work for later. All we need now is *reasonable* proof that the idea is *financially workable*.

Marketing Costs include selling, advertising and promotion. What's a *reasonable* amount? Are there Benchmarks? Try 20 to 25% of your Revenue.

Operating Costs include all your administration and overhead. Another benchmark? Try 12 to 15%. You can easily find benchmark marketing and operating costs for your specific industry.

Subtract Marketing and Operating Costs from Gross Margin to see your estimated Income Before Tax…a good indicator of workability is 15 to 20%.

Remember this is an educated estimate, *a reasonable guess.* It is our *first* test. It's a test that establishes if the idea *might* make good financial sense.

Operating Statement - Estimate Format

Revenue	$100,000	100%
Units: 10,000		
Unit Sales Price: $10		
Less: Cost of Goods	**$45,000**	**45%**
Unit Cost: $4.50		
Gross Margin	**$55,000**	**55%**
Less:		
Marketing Costs	**$23,000**	**23%**
Operating Costs	**$12,000**	**12%**
Income Before Tax	**$20,000**	**20%**

Once this estimate format is "hard wired" into you memory, you'll make mental adjustments automatically to each component as you examine more detailed plans or alternatives.

Now, how about those other important rewards: your personal satisfaction, energizing the *right* people, becoming part of the *right* location. They're just as important as profit!

Case Story: General Electric

Why are we here? "What's in it for you?"

At GE, the question has a simple answer: "We exist to solve problems that can make life better — for our customers, our communities and societies, and for ourselves. We turn innovative ideas into reality."

GE traces its heritage to Thomas Alva Edison. The electrical exhibits at the 1876 Centennial Exposition in Philadelphia marked the beginning of a new era.

As a result, Edison opened a new and well-equipped laboratory in Menlo Park, New Jersey. There he explored the possibilities of the dynamo and other electrical devices he had seen at the Exposition. From his laboratory came perhaps the greatest invention of all – a successful incandescent electric lamp.

Edison established Edison Electric Light Company in 1878. A merger with Thomson-Houston Electric Company in 1892 created the General Electric Company.

Today GE is a diversified technology and services company producing aircraft engines and power generation systems to financial services, medical imaging, television programming and plastics. GE ranks fifth on the annual *Fortune 500*. If ranked separately, all eleven GE businesses would appear on the *Fortune 500*. GE operates in more than 100 countries and employs more than 315,000 people, worldwide.

Just as Thomas Alva Edison changed the world with the power of his ideas, GE honors Edison's core values by turning innovative ideas into reality.

Edison's early business ideas are still part of GE today

Several of Edison's early business ideas are still part of GE today, including lighting, transportation, industrial products, power transmission and medical equipment.

The first GE Appliances – electric fans – were produced as early as the 1890s. A full line of heating and cooking devices was developed in 1907. GE Aircraft Engines, the division's name only since 1987, began its story in 1917 when the U.S. government began its search for a company to develop the first airplane engine "booster" for the fledgling U.S. aviation industry.

Edison's experiments with plastic filaments for light bulbs in 1893 led to the first GE Plastics department, created in 1930.

Jeffrey Immelt, CEO at GE. Every chief executive of GE – there have been only 10 – is expected to put his own stamp on the company, even to radically remake it if necessary.

GE went through one of its rare troughs: Its stock was down from its mid-2000 peak, and in 2001 it failed to continue a long record of double-digit revenue and profit growth. In 2003 the company's revenue grew just 1.5 percent; profit was up only 6 percent. Cost pressures in many old-line GE businesses, from appliances to plastics, were fierce. Immelt saw the threat clearly: "We're all just a moment away from a commodity hell."

GE is making a radical and risky *reinvention* of itself

Today it's clear that Immelt is making a radical and risky *reinvention* of General Electric. Immelt has staked GE's future growth on the force that guided the company at its birth and for much of its history: world-shaking technological innovation.

By learning to manage innovation, Immelt aims to remake GE into a technology powerhouse. And he wants to harness that powerful innovative capability to a more highly developed and systematic marketing organization.

"In the late '90s," Immelt told the press, "we became business traders and not business growers. Today, unceasing reinvention is *the* core commitment at GE. And, to help make it happen, executive compensation is tied to its internal growth.

Immelt believes GE will look like an entirely different company – more entrepreneurial, more science-based, and generating more growth from its own internal operations than by simply seeking to acquire other companies.

GE's Reward Value Driver is simple but ambitious:

Reinvention, managed innovation and continuous improvement will provide a 10 percent per year revenue growth path. Up to 7 percent of added annual revenue will come from internal growth; the balance from acquisitions. An unmistakable challenge and opportunity for the entire organization: Turn your innovative ideas into a reality. And, shareholders see a new, more profitable organization emerging into the 21st century.

Peter Ducker, in his book *Management's Challenges for the 21st Century,* gives us an unmistakable signal as to the underlying reason for Immelt's strategy for GE:

> "The first – and usually the best – opportunity for change is to exploit one's own successes and to build on them."

The challenges of igniting innovation at a colossus like GE are large. But in many ways they aren't very different from the issues all companies, large or small, face when trying to unleash their innovative power.

Here's insight to the "people" ingredient

General Electric, Cobalt Boats, J.M. Smucker, King Arthur Flour Company and Southwest Airlines. These five Case Stories are especially significant when it comes to rewards. The human ingredient of business is deeply woven into the cloth of each company's success.

Each Case Story provides an insight, how rewards create a vision worth following…

General Electric: From its very beginnings, as Thomas Alva Edison was changing the world with the power of his ideas, GE stands out from all the rest with one capability above all others - the ability to *imagine*. The act of imagining at GE is fused with empowerment – "The confidence that what we imagine, we can make happen."

"We exist to solve problems that can make life better — for our customers, our communities and societies, and for ourselves. We turn innovative ideas into reality."

Cobalt Boats: Back in 1970, the town of Neodesha, Kansas enticed Pack St. Clair to move his two-year-old, still-struggling venture from his hometown in nearby Chanute into buildings on a sprawling refinery works vacated by Standard Oil.

It wasn't long before St. Clair understood that he'd tapped into a rich local resource: a solid core of unusual, skilled workers. Folks that were formerly farmers: Each with an unstinting, self-reliant work ethic, a can-do farmer's ingenuity, a deep-seated communal spirit. And perhaps most important of all, *an owner's mindset structured to use Cobalt's resources.*

As a result, Cobalt quality is admired as the outstanding name of the runabout class. They're also the biggest employer and cornerstone of the community.

Do people with special capabilities form part of your Reward Value Driver? Can you attract and keep them with your Core Values?

J. M. Smucker Company – Selected by *Fortune magazine* as the best company to work for in America! The company is run by its co-CEOs, Tim and Richard Smucker.

Orrville, Ohio is a quiet, tidy town 50 miles south of Cleveland. Smucker folks adhere to an extremely simple code of conduct set forth by former CEO Paul Smucker, Tim and Richard's father: Listen with your full attention, look for the good in others, have a sense of humor, and say thank you for a job well done.

Newcomers are often skeptical about the Smucker code. But they quickly learn this "family feel" is for real. It's a throwback to a much simpler time.

If a simple code of conduct works for Smucker, won't it work anywhere?

King Arthur Flour – In 1996, King Arthur launched an Employee Stock Ownership Plan (ESOP), putting ownership of the company in the hands of its employees, everyone at the Round Table.

For almost two centuries five generations of the Sands family have headed King Arthur. Frank E. Sands, II, now Chairman of the Board, told the press, "It seemed only natural to structure ourselves the way King Arthur and his knights did, as a team built on inclusion and collaboration. Today, we are over 160 owners."

The result is a corporate culture of *incredible passion and sincerity*. One that propels King Arthur folks to honor their customers and honor a company they can truly call their own. Some outsiders may scoff at such high ideals in today's cold and indifferent business world. But to them, there is no other way to successfully run a company.

Does your Reward Value Driver involve and nurture important ideals?

Southwest Airlines: While the rest of the industry laid off thousands of people and lost more than $22 billion, Southwest kept every single employee and remained in the black every single quarter. Southwest's core values made it possible to have wide enough margins to take a hit.

Why do competitors find it so hard to copy Southwest's success? Chairman and Founder Herb Kelleher commented, "Listen, we have an incredible esprit de corps here. It's like the Marine Corps. The intangibles have always been more important than the tangibles. Plus we run this company to prepare ourselves for the bad times, which always come in any business."

Does your Reward Value Driver reach for greatness?

Value Driver REWARD Summary:

Think about "reward" in two ways: financial and personal. Without profit, there *is* no business. Prove that the idea is financially workable. Use an "educated estimate." Make it your *first* test. Just as important, develop the corollary rewards: personal satisfaction, energizing the *right* people, becoming part of the *right* location. This involves how your company works and its business model. The challenge: Turn innovative ideas into a reality; Learn to manage innovation; Attract outstanding people.

Task N° 5 – Reward

It's time to identify your Idea's Reward. Go to your **Core Value Proposition Worksheet.**

Reward – What's in it for you? For your Partners or Stockholders? Employees?	

"I am a great believer in luck, and I find the harder I work, the more I have of it." – *Thomas Jefferson*

The Core Value Proposition is what makes your company *unique*. It is not just a set of words, another *traditional* business plan "vision." It provides order and alignment throughout the organization.

The Core Value Proposition incorporates the context of each Value Driver. It creates a clear, solid business model. It describes these values in a brief and understandable fashion. It is the nexus as we proceed to…

- **Prove the Core Value Proposition is workable** – Give life to the idea! Make sure it is financially workable?

- **Use the Core Value Proposition as the core of a compelling business plan** – Tailor its content to a specific communications purpose.

CAUTION: These 3 concepts are TOTALLY different from the Core Value Proposition!

Value Proposition and **Value Based Marketing** are frequently associated with sales strategy and client sales presentations, especially in the software industry. Used in this sense, the focus is *exclusively* upon product or service benefits and advantages.

The **Executive Summary** is another common concept. It forms the introduction of a *traditional* business plan. It is a summary prepared <u>after</u> completing the business plan. Its preparation calls for addressing topics such as Objectives, Mission and Keys to Success.

REMEMBER: These 3 concepts are totally different from the Core Value Proposition.

• • •

The Core Value Proposition Advantage:

The Core Value Proposition is created — then tested — <u>before</u> attempting to write a business plan. Unlike the *traditional* business plan format, it establishes the foundation upon five customer oriented Value Drivers. The process is easier to understand and use *plus* it provides a more complete, long lasting expression of the business-building idea.

The disciplines involved in creating the Core Value Proposition help avoid most of the common plan writing errors: too lengthy or verbose, too complex or just filled with fluff and jargon.

How to weave a Core Value Proposition.

STOP: Before passing "Go", please return to these two Case Stories. Read each carefully so you have their background information clearly in mind.

King Arthur Flour, Target Value Driver

Cobalt Boats, Perception Value Driver

GO: Now read the Core Value Propositions for each company on the following page. Would you say they are complete?

Core Value Proposition Chapter 3 – Target	**King Arthur:** We are a flourmill dedicated to bringing back the American tradition of home baking through a corporate culture of incredible passion and sincerity. A culture that compels us to honor our customers and celebrate a company all our people can truly call their own. We view profit and wealth-creation as the inevitable byproducts of our doing things well. (60 words)
Core Value Proposition Chapter 4 – Perception	**Cobalt Boats** aspire to a single objective: Water bound fun for family and friends. We design and manufacture an unbroken succession of boats that make the best use of technology…boats that incorporate our imagination and innovation in ever-new iterations of nautical science. Cobalt boats represent an uncommon value. Value born of an insistence upon the ultimate importance of details. Details, when seen even from afar, gather toward greatness. (68 words)

Please note your suggestions before turning the page.

Test each Core Value Proposition x Value Drivers

I sensed they were not complete. So I tested each Core Value Proposition to see if it is *really* complete. I matched its content against each of the five Value Drivers. I found problems as indicated with the ✗ my suggested changes are within parenthesis...

| Core Value Proposition: King Arthur Flour: We are a flourmill dedicated to bringing back the American tradition of home baking **(as a complete source of baking products and educational services)** through a corporate culture of incredible passion and sincerity. A culture that compels us to honor our customers, **(folks who are deeply involved with baking, professional bakers and serious baking hobbyists),** and celebrate a company all our people can truly call their own. We view profit and wealth-creation as the inevitable byproducts of our doing things well. (81 words) | ✓ **Nº 1 - Idea: What is it we do for the Customer?** "We help bring back the American tradition of home baking."
 ✗ **Nº 2 - Benefit: What's in it for the Customer?** (a complete source of baking products and educational services)
 ✗ **Nº 3 - Target: Who is the Target?** (Folks who are deeply involved with baking, professional bakers and serious baking hobbyists)
 ✓ **Perception: How do we want to be perceived?** A corporate culture of incredible passion and sincerity
 ✓ **Reward: What's in it for us?** A company all our people can truly call their own; profits and wealth-creation is the inevitable byproducts of our doing things well. |

| Core Value Proposition: **Cobalt Boats** aspire to a single objective: Water bound fun for family and friends. We design and manufacture an unbroken succession of boats **(for those who *own* a "trailerable" boat or who *dream* about owning a boat)** that make the best use of technology…boats that incorporate our imagination and innovation in ever-new iterations of nautical science. Cobalt boats represent an uncommon value **(in construction, comfort and ongoing service)**. Value born of an insistence upon the ultimate importance of details. Details, when seen even from afar, gather toward greatness. (**Our profitability sustains, protects and grows our capabilities**.) (96 words) | ✓ **Nº 1 - Idea: What is it we do for the Customer?** We design and manufacture an unbroken succession of boats that make the best use of technology. ✓ **Nº 2 - Benefit: What's in it for the Customer?** Our boats provide water bound fun for family and friends; and, an uncommon value (in construction, comfort and ongoing service). ✗ **Nº 3 - Target: Who is the Target?** (those who *own* a "trailerable" boat or who *dream* about owning one) ✓ **Perception: How do we want to be perceived?** As an uncommon value. Value born of an insistence upon the ultimate importance of details. Details, when seen even from afar, gather toward greatness. ✗ **Reward: What's in it for us?** (Our profitability sustains, protects and grows our capabilities.) |

Develop The Core Value Proposition
PROVE the Idea is workable!

"Unless commitment is made, there are only promises and hopes... but no plans." Peter Drucker

Gather an Advisory Group...

It's time to think about gathering a group of advisors, a sounding board. People who can help you prove and develop the value of your idea.

Examine your network of friends, business associates, and professionals. You're looking for individuals with valuable industry expertise and insight. People you can call on to help and consult with you as your business idea unfolds.

If you're doing a new business startup, this is the right time to decide on your bank *and* your banker. If you don't already have an interested banker then shop around for one you can involve in your advisory group. This choice and involvement can be critical when it comes time to look for financing.

CAUTION: There's nothing worse than seeking financial help when it's *really* too late! Early on, learn about your bank's loan process, their business plan requirements and application information... *before* you need it.

An advisory group is just as important when you're refocusing or creating a new product for your company. Advisors help you avoid both the pitfalls and politics that are a normal part of most organizations.

Ask advisors to review your Value Drivers and Core Value Proposition. Mark out with them your milestone dates for proving its value, building a compelling business plan and then bringing it to the marketplace.

Most people are flattered to volunteer as an advisor – as long as the time involved is not excessive. Perhaps an occasional advisor's luncheon meeting: prepare a working agenda well in advance.

When meeting with your volunteer advisory group, remember JW Smucker's code of conduct: Listen with your full attention and say thank you for a job well done. Send a "thank you" gift. Pay for the lunch and, perhaps, send a choice bottle of wine!

SCORE, Counselors to America's Small Business

SCORE, known as "Counselors to America's Small Business," is an excellent source of free and confidential small business advice to help you build your business – from idea generation to start-up to ongoing success. The SCORE Association, headquartered in Washington, D.C., is a nonprofit association dedicated to entrepreneurial education and the formation, growth and success of small businesses nationwide.

SCORE's extensive, national network of more than 12,500 working and retired volunteers, are experienced entrepreneurs and corporate executives. These volunteers provide free business counseling and advice as a public service to all types of businesses, in all stages of development...

• At www.score.org – "Ask SCORE e-mail advice online" – select an advisor from 1,200 online counselors.

• Or, free face-to-face counseling at 389 chapter locations. Use the SCORE website to locate the nearest chapter.

Give life to the idea! Make sure it is workable?

It's no surprise! We all seek to reduce or eliminate risk when creating a new business, product or service. We look to market studies: market research, or computer modeling may offer *reasonable* predictions for the success of a Core Value Proposition. What other ways are there to prove an idea is workable?

Fact: There is no substitute for reality.

Your Core Value Proposition can be subjected to a small, controlled *test of reality*. Doing so, you'll confirm… "Nothing ever goes 100% right the first time." Problems emerge that were not expected. Problems that loomed ominously turn out to be slight or non-existent.

If the *test of reality* is successful – *both* problems and opportunities may be uncovered that weren't anticipated while defining the Value Drivers. How and where to change the Core Value Proposition is clear; which strategies prove to be most effective.

• • •

Three ways to Test a Core Value Proposition

No, I'm not suggesting a conventional test market — that might form part of your compelling business plan. But from experience, I've learned there are ways to test a Core Value Proposition in a small, affordable and effective way…here are three suggestions:

Customer Probing: "Probing" is an excellent marketing technique that lets you tune in to your customers and prospects. Learn more about your Value Drivers and Core Value Proposition.

Prepare open-ended questions you'd like to examine with your target customers. Open-ended questions stimulate discussion. For example: "How does this idea fit in to your present needs?" "Of the idea's 4 benefits, which is most important to you?" "Please tell me why?" "What other benefits do you see in this proposition?"

Select 20 to 25 people who are unmistakably in your target market. Visit each and ask for their cooperation evaluating your idea. (Please, no family, friends or relatives!)

Allow each person to read the Core Value Proposition and its Value Drivers. If you can, build or draw a prototype to help visualize your product. Ask your questions. Listen, carefully. Take notes. Examine how the idea could fit into their life. Try to hear what the customer is thinking... *not what you want to hear.*

When you've completed each interview, ask yourself (and make more notes): Does the interview support your Core Value Proposition? Does it cause any concern about a specific Value Driver?

Once you have completed the interviews, write a summary and then examine carefully:

✓ What is the one most important fact you have learned?

✓ Do you *suspect* you need more research?

✓ Are revisions needed to the Value Drivers or the Core Value Proposition?

✓ Do you believe your target market will include enough potential customers?

✓ Are you confident your "guesstimated" numbers will work?

A New Customer Service: Cobalt Boats could reality test a new customer service benefit with a key dealer, one who expressed interest in the Core Value Proposition. They work together providing the new service while gathering proof of its value.

A New Product: King Arthur Flour could reality test a new product's Core Value Proposition with a small group selected from their baking professionals or serious baking hobbyists. Recipes can be tested in their store.

Let your own imagination, customer and market knowledge lead you to an effective reality test. A motel could upgrade just four rooms in a unit and ask for customers' evaluation to the changes. Just make it small, affordable and effective.

Checklist – Marketing and market research sources:

www.brint.com
Business Technology Management & Knowledge Management

www.businessforum.com
Business Forum – resource center for new businesses owners.

www.buzgate.com
Resources to help start, grow and succeed in business

www.ioma.com
The Institute of Management and Administration

www.inc.com
Inc. Magazine - The Resource for Growing Companies

www.business2.com
Business 2.0 Magazine

www.ama.org
American Marketing Association. Find marketing resources and tips.

www.d-source.com
Marketing research directory and search engine

www.market-research-directory.com/
Directory of market research companies

> ### Create a compelling Business Plan
>
> "The best way to predict the future is to create it."
>
> - Peter Drucker

"You'll always miss 100% of the shots you don't take."

What was your decision? "Go!" or "No Go!"

Before making a case for creating a compelling business plan, examine these two conclusions – one of which *might* have occurred while you were working within the Core Value Proposition development process:

✔ **"No Go" – The Idea is NOT workable:** Suppose you discovered during the first steps that the business doesn't make as much sense as you'd anticipated. Say the market isn't growing as fast as you'd thought or gross margins aren't as high as you'd projected. You may decide not to pursue the idea any further. In that case, taking time to create and test your Core Value Proposition has done you a big favor! You saved time, expense and the anguish of writing a business plan for an idea *that wasn't really viable.*

✔ **"Go!" – The Idea is MORE than you imagined:** Conversely, in the course of researching and writing the five Value Drivers you discovered the business opportunity was greater than you'd thought. You adjusted your Value Driver focus. As a result, you changed your approach, rewrote the Core Value Proposition and then proved it to be viable. These new realities make the business opportunity more promising than before.

Four reasons endorse a compelling business plan!

Build upon proven Value Driver's dynamics...

As you put the final touches on the Core Value Proposition, you've already *proven* the validity of your business core values. They are the dynamic force born of your original idea. Creating a compelling business plan extends these dynamics, casting their impact upon the development of each business building activity: from marketing to operations, customer service to finance.

Earn support from others...

A compelling business plan convinces others on the value of your business. When you present a business plan, you're really saying, "Let me sell you on my business." A compelling business plan can easily be compared to marketing materials. Its task is to sell your idea to others. They can be bankers, investors, consultants, employees, suppliers or important customers. It helps you arrange strategic alliances and attract key employees.

Improve your chances of success.

The Core Value Proposition process equips you with knowledge you didn't have before. Writing your plan shapes each detail of building the business, from marketing and operations to finance. You inevitably improve your chances of success.

Increase your self-confidence.

Once you've finished creating your plan – once you've *tasted* success in its presentation – you'll know you're really in control. You know where your business is…where it's going. You have benchmarks to measure your performance. It's that feeling called self-confidence!

Seven FAQ's about writing a Business Plan:

Q: How long should the plan be?

A: Just long enough to tell your story; short enough to keep the reader's attention. Many investors say they'd be happy with a *condensed* format, 5 to 6 pages, no more.

Q: Is there an ideal business plan template or format?

A: Most likely, effective business plans will always be different. It's the plan's communication's objective that creates the difference. A powerful and compelling business plan is custom-built to meet your specific communications objective.

Q: What do you mean by a communications objective?

A: The most frequent communications objective is financial: attracting investment capital or a seeking a bank loan. An equally important objective is taking your plan to your employees, shareholders or partners. Or, you want to reach out with your message to advisors, suppliers and customers. Each plan will be different in its presentation.

Q: How do I custom-build my business plan?

A: Ask yourself these 3 questions:

- **Who is going to receive my plan?** Define your target audience. Think of them as sitting with you around a conference table. Set both the tone and character of your plan and its presentation to meet the occasion.

- **What do they expect from my plan?** Consider each person around the conference table as a potential customer. Make sure their interests and benefits stand out clearly.

- **What do I expect from them?** Your plan is a selling tool, part of a sales presentation. You want to gain their agreement to your proposition. Decide how to reckon if you've earned their acceptance. When you sense it is the *right* moment to "ask for the order" ... Then *ask* for the order!

Q: Do I have to write the plan?

A: The plan must reflect your commitment. If you are developing a project within a group then select the person best qualified to write the plan. Use an editor but make sure the plan is yours in its content, character and tone. *It's your commitment!*

Q: What is most important to investors and bankers?

A: They look at two components *very* carefully: people and cash flow. People make a plan come to life! It's their commitment, talents, capabilities and experience that make the difference. A 3-year cash flow uncovers the quality and reality of business thinking. Best prepared month by month during

Year 1, then quarter-by-quarter. Bankers like to see *how* loan repayment will be made on time. That *makes good sense!*

Q: What cash-flow items are most important?

A: Your "build out" expense, the cost of setting up your business. Working capital requirements and source. Estimated monthly operating expenses. Where is the money coming from? Can your cash flow survive *without* any income to support operating expenses during the first 3 months?

Use SWOT analysis to help form your narrative...

The classic SWOT Analysis is a powerful tool! Use it to stimulate writing a clear and incisive narrative. SWOT (Strengths, Weaknesses, Opportunities and Threats) brings together each of your Value Driver strengths as well as their possible weaknesses, threats or barriers. It helps reinforce the comparative strength, the benefits and advantages of your Core Value Proposition.

You have all the information you'll need for this analysis. Just fashion your own questions using the examples given below as a guide...

Value Driver Strengths:

- **Idea:** What does the Idea DO for the customer. How does the Customer recognize the value of the Idea?

- **Benefits:** The Idea's value for the Customer. Which benefits are outstanding? Given most value? Why?

- **Benefits:** How do the Idea's benefits compare to the competition? Focus on the most important advantages: Is the Idea clearly superior?

- **Target:** How closely defined is your market niche? Can you reach prospects with a reasonable frequency? How will customer and prospect information be managed?

- **Perception:** How strong is your business model? Operations? Production? Customer Service?

- **Reward:** How strong is your financial management?

Value Driver Weaknesses:

- **Idea:** Does any competitor match or provide more than the Idea? How significant is it?

- **Benefits:** How can that benefit be improved to reduce or eliminate weakness?

- **Benefits:** What is the weakest part of the Core Value Proposition?

- **Target:** Is your niche too large? Trying to hit too many people with less than full communications effectiveness?

Value Driver Opportunities:

- **Target:** Where are the best opportunities for your Core Value Proposition?

- **Target:** Will changes in social patterns, population profiles or lifestyle have an effect?

- **Target:** What changes in technology and markets may provide new opportunities?

- **Idea:** What Idea Extensions come from your Target's current characteristics and life styles?

Value Driver Threats (or Barriers):

- **Core Value Proposition:** Could a weakness or threat seriously endanger your business? How? How can this risk be dealt with?

- **Idea:** Is changing technology a threatening factor? To what degree?

- **Perception and Reward:** What are the principal barriers you face? Marketing? People? Money?

- **Reward:** Do you have bad debt or cash-flow problems? How will they be resolved?

- **Benefit and Target:** What is your competition doing? How do they affect the Core Value Proposition?

The Core Value Proposition provides focus to your business plan...

Core Value Proposition

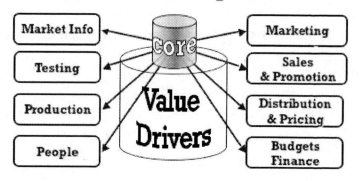

Start composing a *compelling* Business Plan...

Let's call it a story! It's the story of *your* business building idea. Your story is built around clearly stated customer values. You've developed the story using Value Drivers and the Core Value Proposition. Now, your story must be told, presented as a plan, clearly communicated, so it's well understood by all concerned.

It's a short story, not a novel! You've got 5 to 6 pages to tell your story. All stories need a beginning and an end. In between the two you develop your story line, the plot and its narrative.

Open the story. You get only one chance to make a first impression. This old saying carries even more meaning when it comes to your compelling business plan.

The Core Value Proposition will be the most read part of your plan. It is the one component that motivates others to learn more about your business. Please, no more than 80 to 100 words. Consider using the first 10 to 15 words as a kind of headline – words that grab and hold the reader's attention, right from the start!

Develop a clear story line. Connect each of the 5 Value Drivers to their business functions: product or service, your sustainable competitive advantage, market analysis, marketing, operations and finance. Flesh out those tactical details needed for easy understanding. For example…

If you're planning manufacturing: Are production levels, costs and overhead reflected in the Perception and Reward Value Drivers? How about purchasing and inventory management?

Or, a opening a retail store? Is the location fully consistent with the Perception Value Driver, convenient for targeted customers? Are merchandise selection, pricing, markup, inventory turnover rates, promotion and customer service policies all consistent with the Perception Value Driver?

Wrap up the plot. Convert the story line into a financial picture. What do you need to succeed? Sum up how marketing to the customers value perception and acceptance converts into cash flow, profit and return on investment.

A compelling business plan takes time and thought.

Don't underestimate how disciplined you have to be when creating your plan. Get regular feedback from your advisors. Refine...and then refine even more.

Your storyline might look like this...

1. **The Core Value Proposition:** Is the nexus of your compelling business plan. It describes your business in an easy to understand manner. It provides a clear, solid business model, casting its impact upon all segments of the business.

2. **Idea** –Describes your product or service in terms of what it does for the customer. Provides market data and analysis. Indicates current industry trends.

3. **Benefit** – Defines the customer benefits created by the product or service. Compares its advantages with the principal competitors. Indicates potential barriers.

4. **Target** –

   a. **Information Management** – How will you control customer and prospect information? Provide ongoing information within a sales cycle?

   b. **Marketing Communications** – How will your potential customers learn about your product or service? And respond?

    c. **Distribution, Sales Strategy and Pricing** – What practices will you use competing within your business' market?

    d. **Proof of Viability:** Results of market research: Use of a prototype, sales to a small market.

5. **Perception** – Elements that determine how you will be perceived...

    a. **Key Personnel -** Unique or special skills brought to the group: marketing, sales, financial, technical and strategic management.

    b. **Operations** – Describe the business model, HR policies, production and/or service delivery, cost factors, logistics, quality control, and economies of scale.

6. **Financial Data** – What financial assumptions are drawn from the narrative? Capital requirements? Build up or Startup costs? Margins? Operating cost? Key metrics? Start with a simple monthly cash flow projection for 1 year; quarterly for following two years. Include sufficient detail for operational evaluation.

Make your presentation with PowerPoint...

Once you've got your plan in final form, it's just one more step to create a presentation. Let's say you just learned that tomorrow you have 45 minutes to sell your plan to a group of investors.

Set up 10 PowerPoint slides. Using the storyline above, these could be their content...

1. Opening Title Slide

2. The Core Value Proposition

3. Value Driver Summary

4. Competitive Summary

5. Viability Proof

6. Business Model

7. Marketing & Sales

8. Management

9. Financial projections and key metrics

10. Current Status & Timeline

Make your presentation a selling presentation. Don't ask your audience to read the plan. It's there for support and as a take-away. Practice your sales pitch...and then *practice again*. Be prepared for questions and doubts. Don't spend money on fancy covers for your plan. Make copies on ivory or cream colored stock – it's easier to read. Staple diagonally at the top left corner.

Remember Peter Ducker's philosophy...

"The best way to predict the future ...is to create it."

Post Data

Thoughts and suggestions that occurred to me after closing time...

My editor asked me, "What's the purpose of this section? It doesn't seem to fit."

So I responded, Post Data brings forward pertinent memories and facts mixed with a visualization of the future. Hopefully, you will gain perspective of where we are when we think creatively about business development.

Start with a dream...

"You see things and say 'Why'. But I dream things that never were. And I say, "Why not?"

- George Bernard Shaw, *Back to Methuselah used by John F. Kennedy in his Inaugural Address giving start to the Space Age.*

Building a business always starts with a dream, *your dream, your* visualization of a business opportunity, its products or services...things you are going to create. You declare, "Yes, I *will* do that!"

"One man with courage is a majority"
— Andrew Jackson

Marketing is an ever-changing horizon.

There are few absolutes. What was true yesterday may not be true today; and what is true today most likely will not be true tomorrow.

However, within this exciting world of change there are five marketing rules that consistently pass the test of time.

They form part of marketing's core. Understand them. Use them to light your path in the marketing world.

5 Marketing rules that *never* change!

1. **Everything starts (or stops) with the Customer** (the Consumer or User).

2. **The more you know about your Customer**, the more likely it is you can offer the right product, at the right time, at the right place with the right price.

3. **Customers** are the best and least expensive source of new or additional sales.

4. **Customers are NOT all alike.** Pareto's Principle – the 80/20 Ratio – 80% of your Sales & Profits come from 20% of your Customers.

5. **Logic & Emotion** – The Customer's decision to purchase is always guided by a balanced measure of Logic and Emotion.

Looking back is a mirror to see tomorrow!

Communications is the "glue" used in building and binding markets. Markets, today as yesterday, are where buying and selling takes place. What has changed is our ability to reach out, to *communicate* with more people as markets are formed.

Just 8 decades ago there were no national media. Back in the 1920's Radio was in its infancy. KDKA in Pittsburgh PA was the first licensed radio station. Television was an experiment. During the '30's, magazines gained national coverage: TIME, Saturday Evening Post, Colliers, Ladies' Home Journal. Radio networks became a reality from coast-to-coast.

Vast radio audiences got to know and love stars like Bob Hope, Jack Benny and Fred Allen. Soap operas became a daytime staple: listeners followed Stella Dallas, Ma Perkins and My Gal Sunday. "Soaps" provided effective, low cost advertising vehicles for companies like Colgate-Palmolive, P&G and Lever Brothers. Adventures and mysteries abounded: Lux Radio Theater was nighttime fare; Jack Armstrong sold Wheaties, the Shadow sold Blue Coal. It became the perfect sales medium reaching out to millions of customers.

Television became a reality after World War II. Some radio programs successfully moved across to the TV world. Others fell behind and died. A simple 2-minute potato peeler commercial ushered in direct marketing, sales to the consumer. Advertising agencies mastered programming. Later, they learned the art and science of 30-second commercials. The rest is history. Manufacturers reached consumers on an affordable scale as never before.

The automobile helped create thriving suburbs. And new channels of distribution emerged: wholesalers replaced brokers; single store supermarkets opened and grew into chains. Urban department stores spun out suburban branches. Delivery services grew up around this growth and expansion: UPS, the pioneer; much later, FedEx, the innovator.

Richard Sears, founder of Sears Roebuck, started direct mail selling by in the late 1800's. Sears' catalogs effectively reached into rural markets. Soon others followed suit and direct mail catalogs created another important marketplace.

Direct mailers welcomed computers with open arms. New marketing techniques were shaped from an old standby. They recognized the computer's potential to work with increasing numbers of people on a selective, personalized basis.

This is where "marketing" as we know it today was born.

Today, the Internet is gathering new markets around the globe. We are learning totally different and more effective ways to use marketing communications. New markets are being created with an ongoing consumer dialogue. And, we're beginners again – much the same as when Radio first appeared, Magazines became a major medium and then when TV arrived.

Modern marketing is increasingly complex and contains a constantly growing range of activities.

Recommended reading:

Business development classics from my library...

Strategy:

- **Clausewitz on Strategy,** The Boston Consulting Group, John Wiley & Sons, Inc., 2001
- **Serious Play, How the World's Best Companies Simulate to Innovate**, Michael Schrage, Harvard Business School Press. 2000
- **What Really Works,** Nitin Nohria, William Joyce and Bruce Robertson, Harvard Business Review, Reprint R0307C, www.hbr.org
- **Innovation and Entrepreneurship**, Peter F. Ducker, HarperCollins Publishers, 1985
- **Business @ the Speed of Thought,** Bill Gates, Warner Books, 1999
- **Loyalty Rules!** Frederick F. Reichheld, Harvard Business School Press, 2001

Marketing:

- **Beyond Maxi-Marketing,** Stan Rapp & Thomas L. Collins, McGraw-Hill, 1994
- **Strategic Database Marketing**, Arthur M. Hughes, Irwin Professional Publishing, 1994
- **The Discipline of Market Leaders**, Michael Treacy, Fred Wiersema.

Advertising:

- **On the Art of Writing Copy-Third Edition,** Herschell Gordon Lewis, 2004

Cash Management

- Cash Rules – Learn & Manage the 7 Cash Flow Drivers, Bill McGuiness, Kiplinger Books, 2000

Please visit the our website...

www.corevalue-proposition.com

- **Core Value Newsletter:**

  Register for your copy of our monthly newsletter.

- **The Message Board:**

  Ask questions, share your experience or open a new topic about the Core Value Proposition and its five Value Drivers.

- **Our On-Line Services:**

  Learn more about how we help individuals, companies and organizations take advantage of the Core Value Proposition.

- **Book Store:**

  Place your order for additional copies of this book and other recommended reading topics.

- **Corporate Training & Consultants:**

  A fast paced program with supporting learning materials is available for in-house development of the Core Value Proposition. Special discounts and personalization are available for materials. Please contact Jack Hardy at 877/425-4884 for more information.

ISBN 1-41204937-7